ASTRONAUT

Destination: Space
Living on Other Planets

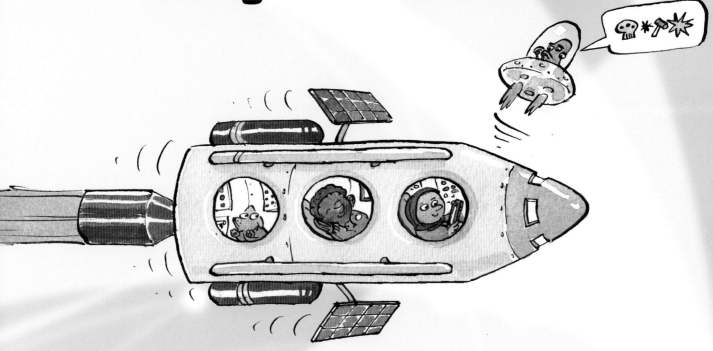

Dr. Dave Williams and Loredana Cunti
art by Theo Krynauw

annick press
toronto + berkeley

Contents

3. Moving Up?

4. Turning Dreams Into Reality

Welcome from Dr. Dave

There are so many great reasons to explore, but the most natural is curiosity. Throughout history, explorers have sought new opportunities, new things to buy and trade, and new lands to discover. The stories of their travels captured the imaginations of other explorers, encouraging them to look even farther for their own adventures.

Dr. Dave Williams

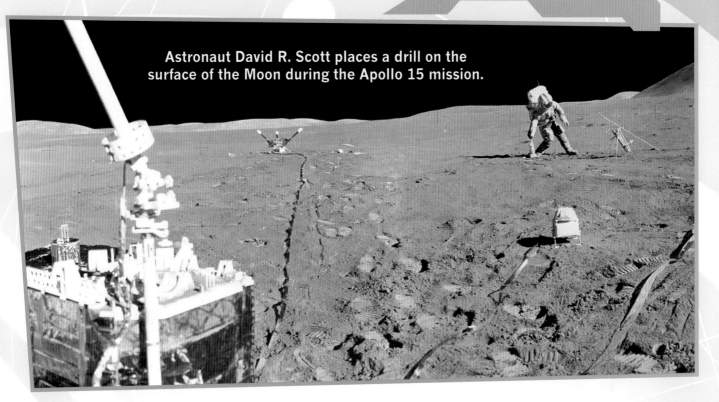

Astronaut David R. Scott places a drill on the surface of the Moon during the Apollo 15 mission.

In the 1960s and '70s, humans started to explore space—in person! We've even walked on the Moon. It's certainly been a great adventure, but space exploration has taught us a lot, too. It's helped us to appreciate our own planet and to understand why Earth is a perfect home for so many different species.

Exploring our solar system has also made us even more curious. Today, we're wondering where else we can go. Could we actually live in outer space? And if so, how would it work? Let's find out!

Astronauts Neil A. Armstrong, Michael Collins, and Edwin E. (Buzz) Aldrin Jr. (left to right) were the first crew to go to the Moon.

Dare to Dream

Long before spacecraft were developed, the dream of exploring our solar system was alive. Our brains came up with ways to get us there, and science fiction became science fact when humans first set foot on the Moon in 1969. Since then, spacecraft have visited Mars, Venus, Saturn's moon Titan, and other comets and asteroids. We've even created a spacecraft that has traveled *beyond* our solar system. So how long until we're living on another planet?

Not So Crazy

That's actually a trick question! Although the idea of humans living in outer space seemed crazy not so long ago, that dream became a reality in 2000 when astronauts started living and working full-time on the International Space Station (ISS). Is your birthday after 2000? If it is, humans have been living in space for your entire life!

So what's next? Can we go farther? Can we stay longer? In the years to come, humans will explore these questions and others. Can we live aboard new space stations orbiting other planets, or can we actually touch down and live on the surface of a planet like Mars? And what can space exploration teach those of us who are comfy and cozy right here on Earth?

Russian, European, and American crew members celebrate astronaut Samantha Cristoforetti's birthday aboard the International Space Station.

The A Team

Dreaming of making space exploration your job? One of these careers might be right for you:

* **astrobiologist:** studies the possibility of life beyond Earth
* **astronaut:** lives and works in space
* **astronomer:** studies the universe and all objects in it
* **astrophysicist:** studies life cycles of objects in the universe

Astrophysicist Jedidah Isler studies blazars (extremely large black holes) in distant galaxies.

Life on Earth

First Things First

The idea of finding a home somewhere else in our solar system is pretty amazing, but we can't just pick up and leave. Turns out that living creatures are complicated . . . and have some pretty big needs.

It's Alive!

What do we mean when we say something is "alive"? A whale, a carrot, a flea, and the bacteria that make you sick are alive, just like you. Why? Big, small, or microscopic, living things are all made up of tiny building blocks called cells, use a fuel (like food) to make energy, can grow, multiply in some way (such as having babies), and can change themselves.

A whale, a carrot, a flea, and bacteria don't look like they have anything in common, but they do—they're all living things.

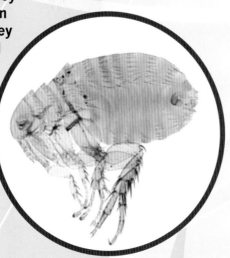

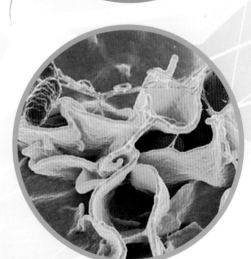

Meet the New Kid

If Earth were only one day old, then the first forms of life appeared at about 4:00 a.m. These microscopic one-celled bacteria got a little bigger and more complicated, but it took all the way until 8:30 p.m. before sea plants developed. Twenty minutes later, sea animals like jellyfish joined them. And just before 10:00 p.m. (past your bedtime!), land plants arrived. Finally, at 1 minute and 17 seconds before midnight, humans showed up. Let's party!

Lots of Living Things

There are more living things on Earth than we can count, but we do know that the planet is home to about 8 million different species. In terms of numbers, the springtail beats all. These insect-like critters are smaller than a pinhead, but they're literally everywhere. Ants come a close second, acting like tiny-but-mighty managers of Earth's surface. And there are more different kinds of beetles than any other living thing. Their jobs, including pollination, are so important that most plants couldn't survive without them. Who knew?

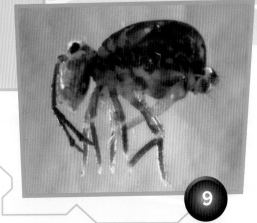

This tiny springtail is almost too small to see, but huge numbers of them live everywhere in soil and other natural ground.

The Perfect Planet

Whether we're talking about bacteria or beetles or humans, Earth is the only place in our solar system that we know can currently support life. Why? Conditions here are just right!

The Soup of Life

When astronomers want to know if another planet can support life, the first thing they look for is liquid water. Liquid is needed for the kinds of chemical reactions that living things depend on, like digestion. And water is the perfect liquid because it *stays* liquid under many conditions and it dissolves things. Earth's surface is about 71 percent water. No shortage of the stuff here!

Oceans and seas make up over 95 percent of the world's water.

Goldilocks and the Sun

Life also needs energy. Our biggest energy source is the sun. The sun's light and heat reach all planets in our solar system, but some get too much and others don't get enough. Earth is just the right distance from the sun. Enough light reaches us for plants to grow, and the temperature is not too hot or too cold— just like the baby bear's porridge in the Goldilocks story!

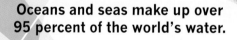

Scientists exploring the possibility of life in our solar system search for planets or moons in what we call the "Goldilocks Zone"—where the temperature is just right for liquid water to exist.

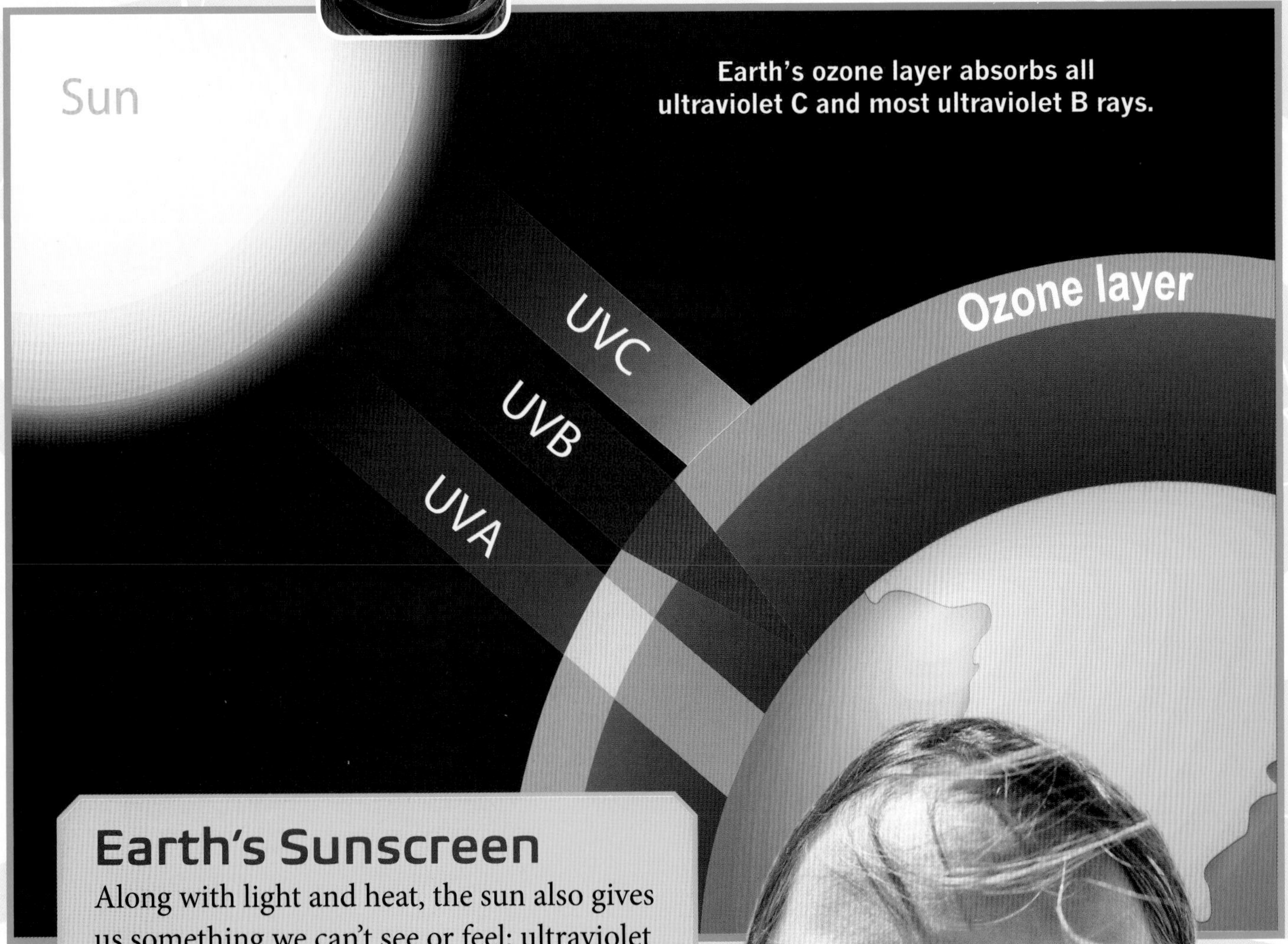

Sun

Earth's ozone layer absorbs all ultraviolet C and most ultraviolet B rays.

UVC

UVB

UVA

Ozone layer

Earth's Sunscreen

Along with light and heat, the sun also gives us something we can't see or feel: ultraviolet radiation, or UV rays. These rays are good in small doses, but if we get too much of them, we'd burn to a crisp. Luckily, a layer of gases surrounds Earth to protect us from these damaging rays. It's the ozone layer, and it traps most of the sun's UV rays before they reach us.

Sunscreen or sunblock stops the ultraviolet A and B rays from burning our skin.

11

When we breathe out on cold days, it's like we can "see" the air, though what we're really seeing is water molecules.

A Is for Atmosphere

Underneath the ozone layer is a blanket made up of . . . air. Even though we can't see it, smell it, or taste it, we definitely need it. The three main gases in Earth's air—oxygen, nitrogen, and a little bit of carbon dioxide—are just perfect for life. Too much carbon dioxide would poison us, but a small amount helps to keep Earth at the right temperature.

We need the oxygen to breathe. Our bodies use that oxygen and turn some of it into carbon dioxide, which plants then take in to produce and release oxygen. And around and around we go.

Earth's Velcro

Holding that airy blanket of atmosphere in place is one more thing that makes Earth such a great place to live: gravity. Gravity pulls in everything that comes close enough. And that's what keeps us from floating away!

12

The Perfect Recipe

It turns out that Earth has the right ingredients in the right quantities to make life possible. Just enough heat to keep water liquid, enough light for plants to grow, and a pinch of carbon dioxide to keep us from freezing or evaporating. If you add all of these things together, you get the perfect climate. Voilà!

Earth's Force Field

Have you ever tried to hold two magnets together? They push themselves apart, making it nearly impossible. That's what happens when the solar wind—tiny charged particles given off by the sun—gets close to Earth. The molten iron deep inside Earth's core acts like a magnet and deflects them, like a giant force field. This protects Earth's atmosphere from being destroyed by the solar wind.

The Earth's magnetic field (the blue lines) pushes away the sun's harmful solar wind (the orange lines).

Space agencies are exploring the idea of creating a magnetic field around spacecraft to keep crews safe from cosmic radiation. Stay tuned!

So, Why Leave?

Humans have a built-in desire to explore. And that's a good thing! Exploring has helped us understand our planet and its place in the universe. But there are other reasons to explore, too.

Treasure Hunt

In the past, when people went exploring, they discovered treasures they hadn't been expecting to find. Entirely new continents! Gold and tomatoes in South America! Copper in Africa! Tea in China!

Space has been called "the final frontier" in the movies, meaning it's the last truly new place to explore. Our curiosity makes us wonder: What's on other planets? Will we find more gold or silver or lead? Or will we find a mineral that we've never seen before? Maybe it will be very, very useful. So astronauts keep exploring, hoping to find new treasures.

Real-life spaceships might not look like the ones we see in movies, but they will allow us to explore other planets.

A Little More Room, Please

People have often traveled to new countries when their home country has become too crowded. As Earth's population grows, some scientists are looking beyond our planet's borders for more room. Imagine having a whole empty planet, or two, to live on! If we could find a way to use the resources on other planets and also make other planets livable, then humans would have unimaginable space. We could also make more room, and more resources, for the people left on Earth.

Exploring other planets may give us a possible solution to overcrowded cities.

Evacuate!

Is it possible that something might one day *force* us to leave Earth? An asteroid strike? Rising sea levels? A deadly disease? Water or food shortages? Writers and moviemakers might like to imagine a forced evacuation, but for now, that's all it is: imagination.

Know the Neighborhood

Looking for Locations!

If your family wanted to move to a new country, or even a new city, your parents would do a lot of research first. Space agencies do the same thing. For many years, they've been sending spacecraft to explore the eight planets in our solar system.

An illustration of the *Venus Express* circling our rocky neighbor Venus.

The Rocky Planets

You don't have to be a rocket scientist to understand why the four planets closest to the sun—Mercury, Venus, Earth, and Mars—are called the "rocky planets." They're mostly rock and metal and have solid surfaces. Could one of these rocky planets be a new home someday?

Jupiter's surface area is over 121 times bigger than Earth.

Jupiter

Saturn

Uranus

Neptune

Earth

Venus

Moon

Mars

Mercury

Pluto

The Giants

The four outer planets are known as "giants"—and we really mean *giant*. You could fit 1,300 Earths into Jupiter, the largest planet in the solar system.

Jupiter and Saturn are "gas giants." Why? Because they're mostly made up of enormous clouds of gases such as hydrogen and helium. They do have small cores, but they're liquid, not solid.

Uranus and Neptune are "ice giants." They're not made of solid ice but of frozen gases and liquids such as water, ammonia, and methane. These are heavier than hydrogen and helium, but still not solid.

Living on one of the gas or ice giants would be hard to imagine. Because they are made of gas, there's no surface to land, walk, or build on. Looks like we need to keep exploring!

Rocky Road

What has space exploration taught us about the possibility for life on the rocky planets?

Mercury

Mission Log: *Mariner 10*; *MESSENGER* probe

What We Know: Weak gravity and no atmosphere count as two strikes against Mercury, the solar system's smallest planet. It's also very hot! During rotation, temperatures on the sun side can be 28 times hotter than on Earth, and the sun is 7 times brighter than we're used to. But there might be ice (and therefore water) near the north and south poles, which are always in shadow.

Verdict: Three strikes, you're out.

In this colorized photo of Mercury's north pole, the red areas are hot, while the shadowy purple areas in the craters are frigid.

Venus

Mission Log: *IKAROS* and *Akatsuki*; *Venus Express*

What We Know: Life on Venus would be like living in a very hot oven. Venus is the hottest planet in the solar system. Its dense air is a choking mixture of poisonous acid gases that are strong enough to dissolve a space suit. Its gravity is about as strong as ours, but that's not enough to make it a potential home away from home.

Verdict: Zero-percent chance.

In this illustration of Venus's surface, lightning snakes down from clouds of sulfuric acid.

Mars

Mission Log: MAVEN mission; ExoMars Trace Gas Orbiter mission

What We Know: Water has been found in Martian soil, and the planet isn't extremely hot. It has enough sunlight to create energy, and while its gravity is weak, it might have just enough for humans. But its thin atmosphere can't protect it from the sun's occasional blasts of high-energy radiation or the violent storms those blasts create.

Verdict: The most likely new home for humans? Check out pages 32–35 for more.

So far, many of the missions exploring our solar system haven't had astronauts on board. This allows the spacecraft to go farther into space and stay longer.

Out of Gas

The gas giants may be way out there, but that hasn't kept us from exploring.

Jupiter

Mission Log: *Juno*; *New Horizons*

What We Know: Jupiter's gassy atmosphere constantly changes, which causes storms that are wider than Earth! One storm has been raging for over 300 years, and massive cyclones swirl over the south pole.

Verdict: Too stormy to stay.

An artist illustrates how the *Juno* spacecraft leaves Jupiter.

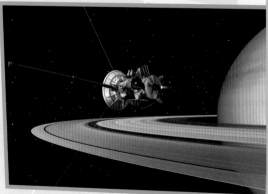

The *Cassini-Huygens* spacecraft entering Saturn's orbit, as imagined by a NASA artist.

Saturn

Mission Log: Cassini-Huygens mission; *Voyager 1* and *2* flybys

What We Know: If you thought Jupiter was stormy, try Saturn. Winds can be 4.5 times faster than the strongest hurricane-force winds on Earth. Then there are the planet's lightning bolts, which are more than 1,000 times stronger than ours.

Verdict: Hold on to your hat—and give this planet a pass!

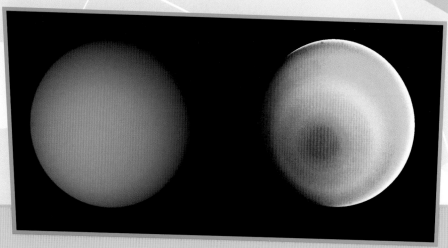

Uranus as seen by the *Voyager 2* spacecraft, in true color (left) and using colored photo filters (right).

Uranus

Mission Log: *Voyager 2* flyby

What We Know: Uranus is the coldest planet in the solar system. And because it's tilted on its side, it has very strange seasons. For half of its "year"—which is 84 Earth years long—the north pole faces the sun while the south pole is in total darkness. For the other half, the poles change places. So, no matter where you lived, your winter would be more than 20 years of darkness.

Verdict: Nope—much too cold and dark.

Neptune

Mission Log: *Voyager 2*

What We Know: Because Neptune is the farthest planet from the sun and Earth, it's hard for us to observe. The only spacecraft to visit was *Voyager 2*, and it took 12 years to get there! Neptune has a thick atmosphere, and an "ocean" of water and ammonia crushes down toward its center. This creates enough pressure to form solid diamonds that whip around in the solar system's fastest winds.

Verdict: Not likely we're going to get there.

An engineer works on the *Voyager* spacecraft.

Tops for Terrestrials

So far, the world's space-faring nations have sent more than 180 probes to explore our solar system. Thanks to their work, we now have a better idea of the top spots in our solar system that might someday support life.

Enceladus

(The sixth-largest moon of Saturn)

Why There? It has fresh clean water ice over a saltwater ocean, plus a lot of the chemicals needed to make life.

Travel Time: 7 years

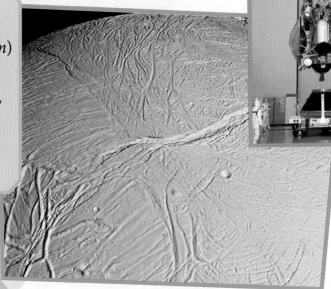

The *Cassini* spacecraft (inset) took this close-up of Enceladus, which shows the many folds, craters, and fractures on the moon's surface.

The *Huygens* probe photographed the surface of Titan for the first time.

Titan

(Saturn's largest moon)

Why There? You would need to wear only a breathing mask on Titan because of its thick atmosphere, which would also protect you from the sun's harmful radiation rays.

Travel Time: 7 years

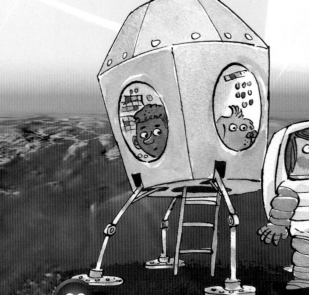

Europa

(One of Jupiter's 69 moons)

Why There? If we could break through Europa's icy crust, we'd find a salty ocean very similar to Earth's.

Travel Time: 5–6 years

This illustration shows what we might see if we could break through Europa's icy surface. Jupiter (right) looms in the background and Io (middle) is brightly visible.

Mars

Why There? The water in Martian soil or its polar ice caps might be able to support life.

Travel Time: 7–10 months

Io

(Another moon of Jupiter)

Why There? Io's thin atmosphere could protect us from radiation, and its many lava tubes could contain life-friendly chemicals.

Travel Time: 6 years

Moon

Why There? We've been there before and it's close to home. We could learn a lot about living on other planets by trying it out on the Moon first.

Travel Time: A few days

NASA has discovered six Earth-like planets in the Milky Way galaxy. These rocky planets are all in the "Goldilocks Zone," where surface water can exist in liquid form. Could they be a possible future home?

3

Enceladus & Titan

Let's take a closer look at those "top spots" for life, starting with two of Saturn's moons—Enceladus and Titan.

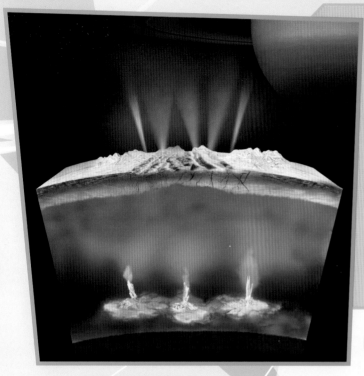

Water jets on Enceladus might be both underwater and on the surface.

Icy Geysers on Enceladus

Saturn's moon Enceladus is small—480 kilometers (300 miles) across, or about the distance between New York and Washington, DC. Ice covers its surface, but near its south pole you can see long blue cracks. Icy droplets and cold moisture squirt out of these cracks into space. The *Cassini* space probe discovered that an ocean lies under the ice.

Winter Camping

If you want to set up camp on Enceladus, the south pole is the place to go. Though the sun is too far away to provide warmth, Saturn's gravity keeps the water below moving around, so it doesn't freeze. You could tap into this energy by drilling through the ice. You might even find some life down there!

TIPS FOR TOURISTS

Most Likely Life-Form: Cold-water microorganisms
What to Pack: A pair of skates
Top Attraction: Playing hockey across a planet-wide rink

24

A view of Saturn could look like this if you were to stand on Titan.

Hazy, Crazy Titan

You've been traveling through space for years and need a break. Where to go? Try Titan! With its thick atmosphere, you're safe from space radiation. You can relax by the shores of a methane lake and gaze through the orange haze at Saturn. You can't miss it—it fills between a third to half of the sky.

That foggy atmosphere is heavier than Earth's air, so you can walk around without a pressurized space suit, but you'll need a helmet with air to breathe. Titan's weak gravity also makes it easy to jump. Before you leave, look for a good high sand dune. Then take a big jump and slowly glide down. Whee!

Life could get lonely on Enceladus and Titan—a message sent home would take at least 1 hour and 12 minutes to arrive. No high-speed Wi-Fi here!

TIPS FOR TOURISTS

Most Likely Life-Form: Methane-loving bacteria lake swimmers
What to Pack: Your parachute
Top Attraction: Hang gliding

Next stop? Jupiter's moons Europa and Io.

Planet Iceberg

Europa looks like a solid ball of ice, but photographs taken by the *Galileo* probe show something surprising: a web of crisscrossing lines. The only other place in the solar system with the same cracked ice is our frozen Arctic Ocean. Beneath Europa's ice is a water ocean that some believe is the most suitable place to search for life in our solar system. Is the ice floating on a salty sea, like one enormous iceberg? What could be living underneath?

Here's another interesting question: If there's water under the ice, why isn't it frozen, too? The sun's warmth probably can't get through, so heat would have to come from Europa's core. There might even be cracks in the seafloor with mineral-rich hot springs, just like those on the bottom of Earth's oceans.

A photo taken by the *Galileo* spacecraft shows cracks crisscrossing the surface of Europa. (inset) This illustration shows water vapor bursting through a crack.

Take me to your leader!

TIPS FOR TOURISTS

Most Likely Life-Form: Deep-sea bacteria
What to Pack: Your scuba gear!
Top Attraction: The view—Jupiter would look 24 times larger than our Moon

Extreme Io

Jupiter's fourth-largest moon, Io, is a land of fire and ice. Temperatures here can be hot enough to keep lava liquid or almost twice as cold as it's ever been on Earth. That's extreme! But under Io's rocky crust, there might still be enough water and energy-producing chemicals for microbes (microscopic living things) to be alive.

Voyager 1 captured this image of a volcano erupting on Io.

Living in Lava Tubes

Io has about 400 active volcanoes—the most in our solar system. All that lava travels from Io's core to its surface through cracks. And when it hardens, it forms cave-like tubes. Scientists believe there could be lava tubes on Io and that these caves would be a good spot for living things, just like lava tubes on Earth. The thick walls would provide protection from the sun's radiation, trap moisture, and supply life-giving chemicals from the sulfurous lava.

TIPS FOR TOURISTS

Most Likely Life-Form: Simple life-forms that only "wake up" when nutrients arrive
What to Pack: Your heat-resistant space suit
Top Attraction: Volcano watching!

27

Moon Mission

So far, 12 astronauts have been to the Moon. They've even lived on its surface for three days. What would it take to live there full-time? The first thing we'd need is someplace to call home. Right now, there are two options: bring one or build one.

Pack the Tent!

The Bigelow Expandable Activity Module (BEAM), an inflatable habitat or space "tent," has been on the International Space Station since 2016, having traveled there in the cargo area of the *Dragon* spacecraft. It grew to five times its folded size when a robotic arm unpacked it and it was inflated with air from the space station. It's like living in a big balloon made from the material used in some space suits. Similar models could work as a base camp on the Moon's surface.

NASA staff get a tour of fully inflated space tents.

Spaceships aren't very big, so whether you're taking a tent or tools, your cargo has to be as small and lightweight as possible.

NASA astronauts test how a 3-D printer works in microgravity.

3-D It Yourself

Another way to make a home on the Moon is to build one! Astronauts could do this using 3-D printers, which are already being used on Earth. A 3-D printer could make tools or bricks out of regolith, the rocky material found on the Moon. The "bricks" can then be used to build a habitat or a protective dome to place over an inflatable habitat.

Going Underground

Setting up a space "tent" underground is another possibility. In 2017, the Japanese *Kaguya* orbiter discovered a giant lava tube under the Moon's surface—it's more than 50 kilometers (31 miles) long and is 91 meters (300 feet) below the surface. Inside, a habitat would be safe from flying asteroids and radiation. The Moon and Mars are both covered in regolith, a volcanic rock. Earth's soil is a kind of regolith, but it's mixed with tons of organic remains, like composted plants.

Lunar Living

Once your lunar home is set up, you would need
a few basics: air, water, and food.

Take a Deep Breath

Astronauts living on the Moon would breathe air
in their habitats and oxygen in their space suits.
But they can't carry all the air they'd need. Luckily,
the Moon's rocky regolith contains both oxygen and
hydrogen. Space planners are working on ways to
extract these elements and turn them into forms we can
use, like breathable air and drinkable water.

Road Trip!

Once we're on the Moon, we'd want to look
around. Today's Space Exploration Vehicles look
more like luxury RVs than the "dune buggies"
astronauts used in the 1970s. One vehicle design
has 12 wheels and can take two astronauts
on road trips lasting several days. And their
pressurized, closed cabins make it safe to take off
space suits.

**This model for a
rover has an electric
motor powered by
solar panels. The
back section is a full
laboratory that can
disconnect from the
front section.**

What's for Dinner?

If we're planning to stay awhile, we won't be able to pack all the food we need. Thankfully, scientists have designed collapsible "greenhouses." These tube-shaped buildings need to be buried underground to protect the plants from deadly solar flares, bits of flying meteorites, and radiation. Robots would tend the plants, which could grow in either water or soil.

NASA has tested growing plants underwater. If there's enough light and the temperature's right, they grow—and you don't have to worry about watering them!

TIPS FOR TOURISTS

Most Likely Life-Form: The *Apollo* lunar samples didn't reveal any Moon microbes. The search continues.

What to Pack: Your selfie stick: "Look, Mom! That's me and Earth!"

Top Attraction: Jumping! You can leap up to 3 meters (10 feet) on the Moon thanks to gravity that's one-sixth of what it is on Earth.

Destination: Mars

Mars has excited space adventurers for a long time. It's like Earth in some important ways: it has water, seasons, and a day that's a similar length to an Earth day.

Are We There Yet?

Mars is far! To reduce travel time, spacecraft would be launched when Mars is closest to Earth in its orbit. Still, it would take seven to ten months to get there. What would happen to our bodies during that journey? Without gravity, every day would be a workout day. Exercise stops the loss of muscle strength, keeps bones strong, and maintains fitness for those first space walks after landing! If only humans could hibernate!

Landing Armor

Mars has an atmosphere—which is a good thing when it comes to living there. But that atmosphere also makes landing tricky. Something as fast as a spaceship creates heat when it rubs up against air particles. You would need a heavy-duty heat shield to protect your spaceship from burning to a crisp. And since the air on Mars isn't thick enough to slow you down, you would need powerful jets, parachutes, or an airbag to help apply the brakes.

In this artist's vision of landing on Mars, rockets slow a space vehicle down so that it can gently lower a rover.

An illustration of the NASA X-38 docking at the ISS, in preparation for returning the crew to Earth.

Be Prepared

Before humans ever set foot on Mars's red soil, missions would be sent to deliver food and supplies, extra space suits and equipment, a backup habitat, a rover, and an Assured Crew Return Vehicle (ACRV)—a spacecraft that can be used to return to Earth. Additional supplies would go with the crew when they leave. And once the crew is living on Mars, resupply spacecraft would be sent every few months. Talk about being prepared!

Some believe that living on the red planet isn't so far away and that we could be there by 2030.

Life on the Red Planet

Because it takes so long to get to Mars, we need to plan to stay awhile. What would we need to live there for years, or even permanently?

Grow Your Own

Packing food is fine for short trips, but Mars dwellers would have to grow their own. To start, food could be grown in pressurized greenhouses on the planet's surface. Carbon dioxide from Mars's atmosphere could feed the plants, and the plants would then make oxygen for us to breathe. It's possible that plants could be grown using water from one of Mars's poles or from the soil once it has been purified.

Russian cosmonaut Maxim Suraev
harvests lettuce on the ISS.

Europe's space program experiments with growing the green bacteria, spirulina, in Congo. Spirulina turns carbon dioxide into oxygen and is resistant to radiation. It's also an excellent source of protein.

Go Big or Go Home

Over a few decades, we could build bigger greenhouses—big enough to hold parks, forests, and lakes. These mini-ecosystems would need the protection of pressurized domes, caves, or underground caverns to survive. But we'd also have to start "terraforming" to prepare for the far-distant future. Terra-what? *Terraforming* means changing the actual planet to be more Earth-like. So how do we do that?

* **Step 1:** "Plant" microorganisms that can use Martian air and release oxygen and nitrogen—the kinds of gases that will create a cozy Earth-like atmosphere.

* **Step 2:** Once the atmosphere is thick enough, plant dark seeds and algae. These will absorb sunlight so that the chilly planet will eventually warm up.

* **Step 3:** Wait. The algae and dark plants will slowly break down to form nutrient-rich soil. After this, our great-great-great-great-great-great-great- (and more greats) grandchildren might be able walk in the Martian woods.

TIPS FOR TOURISTS

Most Likely Life-Form: Microbes that love eating iron-rich regolith

What to Pack: Board games (for waiting out the dust storms)

Top Attraction: Surfing the sand dunes

Moon or Mars?

So where will we end up living first—the Moon or Mars? There are lots of things to consider before that decision is made.

Big or Small?

The *Columbia* spacecraft that carried three astronauts to the Moon in 1969 was the size of a small car inside. It's hard to sit in a car for 260 days! A Mars spacecraft would have to be at least six times larger than the unmanned probes we've already sent. And a Mars habitat would have to be bigger and stronger than either the ISS or a Moon habitat. Not only would we be staying longer, but Mars has just 37 percent of Earth's gravity, and staying longer means more living space.

The kind of spacecraft that could take astronauts to Mars could look like this one.

The Mars Exploration Rover *Spirit* took this photo of boulders and dust on Mars.

Different Dust

Both the Moon and Mars are covered in dust. Moon dust is sharp and jagged, while the wind and water on Mars have made its dust round and polished. Moon dust jams engines, clogs up the wheels of lunar rovers, and chews through space suits. So, vehicles and space suits would have to be designed differently, depending on whether they're meant for the Moon or Mars.

Cliffs and Craters

Driving around on the Moon would be bumpy, but Mars is really challenging. The planet is home to the highest mountain, the deepest and longest valley, and the largest volcanoes in our solar system. Rovers would need special tires to survive conditions on Mars.

A planetary rover developed by the Pacific International Space Center for Exploration Systems (PISCES) gets tested on the volcanic rock of Hawaii.

The Verdict?

The Moon is close enough for a quick holiday, but Mars is for space travelers who plan to stay. Some people think we should go back to the Moon to learn how to manage the risks of going to Mars. Others think we should focus on going to Mars.

Already There?

What if our future lives in space weren't on a planet but in . . . space? This isn't such a strange idea. We've already been living in space for almost 20 years, on the International Space Station.

Piece by Piece

In November 1998, Russia launched the *Zarya*, a self-contained module that became the first part of the International Space Station. More modules were sent up and attached in orbit. The ISS is now as long as a football field, with about as much livable space as a five-bedroom house, including two bathrooms and a gym. Sixteen countries work together to build, maintain, and occupy it.

Astronaut Rick Mastracchio attaches a new segment to the ISS during one of his space walks.

The ISS is the most expensive and complicated single thing ever built in space, and the largest human-made structure in space!

Life "Up There"

The ISS orbits Earth every 90 minutes, so the crew sees 16 sunrises and sunsets every Earth day. The crew's 12-hour workday is spent conducting experiments and cleaning and fixing the station. Every day is planned well in advance, even years before, by teams on Earth. But life on the ISS isn't all work. Friday nights are movie nights—sometimes Saturdays, too!

Crew on the ISS relax for an evening to watch *Star Wars: The Last Jedi*.

Shift Work

The ISS crew "changes shift" every three to six months, but there have been at least three (and as many as thirteen) astronauts living on board since November 2000. This means the ISS is home to the longest continuous human presence in Earth's orbit.

From 2015 to 2016, Scott Kelly and Mikhail Kornienko set the record for the longest stay on the ISS, at 340.4 days. Because we age slower in space, when Captain Kelly returned to Earth, he was younger than his identical twin (by 13 milliseconds).

Bye!

Hi!

Astronauts Scott Kelly and Mikhail Kornienko mark their 300th day in space.

Space Cities

Living on the ISS has taught us a lot about how to live in space. What if we could build larger and larger space stations, big enough for hundreds of people?

Astronaut Leland Melvin removes part of the Water Recovery System that is being improved to recycle all water used on the ISS, including sweat and urine.

Extreme Sustainability

Earth cities rely on resources far outside their boundaries, like farms and rivers that might be hundreds or even thousands of miles away. But space cities would need to be almost completely independent of Earth's resources. Everything, such as oxygen, water, and food, would have to be recycled or reused as much as possible. Space farms would have to produce the maximum amount of food possible— no room for weeds or wasted veggies. And everyone would need to compost; the goal would be to make all trash biodegradable.

Resistance Required

One of the big challenges to living in space is the lack of gravity. Over years and decades, a lack of gravity would turn our bodies into useless blobs. If you were born in space, how would you grow up healthy and strong? One plan for making "fake gravity" is to build a habitat that rotates, like a wheel around an immobile center. The rotation provides a force for your body to work against, like when you're in a car making a fast turn.

The Stanford Torus is one design for a space colony. This illustration shows a rotating ring around a motionless central hub and its reflection in a giant solar mirror.

To film the science fiction movie *2001: A Space Odyssey*, a giant "Ferris wheel" was built to mimic the rotating ring needed for space living.

Space Public Transit

Rockets need a lot of fuel to break away from the strong pull of Earth's gravity. This makes them too expensive for sending people and supplies into space regularly. Instead, space elevators or "beanstalks" could work like buses to space. These "trolley cars" would travel along a cable anchored at the equator at one end and, at the other, a heavy landing pad parked outside Earth's orbit. The trick is developing a cable that's strong enough. Pure carbon graphene might be the answer.

Danger Zone

Whether it's on the Moon, Mars, or a floating space city, life anywhere other than on Earth won't be easy. For humans, space is a "hostile environment." That means it's dangerous for us to be there.

Weightless Worries

Traveling between homes on Earth and in our solar system would be hard on our bodies. When we travel to space, we enter different "gravity fields." In between planets, there's no gravity at all—we're weightless. But other planets have their own gravity, different from what we're used to on Earth. All of this switching back and forth can weaken our bones and muscles, affect our ability to balance, and even hurt our hearts and eyes.

Astronaut Rhea Seddon spins Martin Fettman in a rotating chair to test him for motion sickness.

Living in a small space means that we share everything—even the tiny bacteria that live on our bodies!

Crews on the ISS need to get used to working and living in small spaces.

So Lonely

The journey into space can be long—and lonely. Only a few astronauts can travel at one time, and spacecraft are pretty small. Homes on other planets will likely be small, too. That can be difficult for human beings, who are used to having lots of space and lots of company. Scientists know that being isolated and stuck in a tiny space can make us grumpy, sad, and tired.

Solar Rays

The Earth has a force field that helps to protect us from space radiation. Other planets aren't so lucky. If we can't figure out a way to shield ourselves, we could experience an increased risk of cancer and damage to our nervous systems. Scary stuff!

Practice Makes Perfect

How could we protect ourselves from the risks of living in space? Practice makes perfect—and space agencies have come up with amazing ways to practice for life on another planet.

Let's Pretend

Earth is human-friendly, but it can be extreme, too. Scientists believe some conditions in deserts, oceans, volcanoes, and the North and South Poles are similar to conditions in space. That's why they use these spots for "analog missions"—also known as "playing pretend." Analogs help to test space suits, tools, rovers, habitats—and even humans—to learn lessons that will help future space explorers.

HI-SEAS Adventure

In September 2017, six "astronauts" emerged from a habitat on Hawaii's Mauna Loa volcano. They'd been inside for eight months. The HI-SEAS analog studied how humans would respond to a mission to Mars. The "crew" dressed in space suits and traveled in teams whenever they left the small dome. They shared one shower and two toilets. They ate canned and freeze-dried food, and vegetables they grew themselves. And they wore sensors to measure their moods. NASA will use what it learned to prepare for a real mission to Mars.

The landscape found on the Mauna Loa volcano resembles one that astronauts might find on Mars.

Inside the HERA habitat (left). The NEEMO 9 crew (right) prepare for a night dive: (clockwise from top right) Dr. Dave, Ronald J. Garan Jr., Nicole P. Stott, and Tim Broderick.

Amazing Analogs

There are always analog missions on the go. Here are a few happening right now:

* NEEMO sends scientists to live in Aquarius, the world's only undersea research station. The ocean floor is a great place to learn how to spacewalk!

* The Haughton Mars Project is on Devon Island in Canada's Arctic. The polar desert setting and harsh climate make it a perfect spot to test communications systems and vehicles.

* HERA is a three-story habitat at the Johnson Space Center in Texas. It's used to explore the effects of isolation, confinement, and remote conditions on astronauts.

The Haughton Mars Project team cheers outside their Arctic base station. They tested a drill that is being developed to work on Mars.

Go Farther, Stay Longer

The huge distances between Earth and deep space are another challenge to overcome. To make living in space a reality, we need to figure out how to get there faster and stay longer.

NEXT Up

The NASA Evolutionary Xenon Thruster (NEXT) engine might be the answer. Using the latest technology to increase thrust—the force that propels a spacecraft—these engines will accelerate to speeds five times faster than today's spacecraft are capable of traveling. The plan is to hit 144,840 kilometers (90,000 miles) per hour. Another bonus? The NEXT engines use much less fuel than today's models.

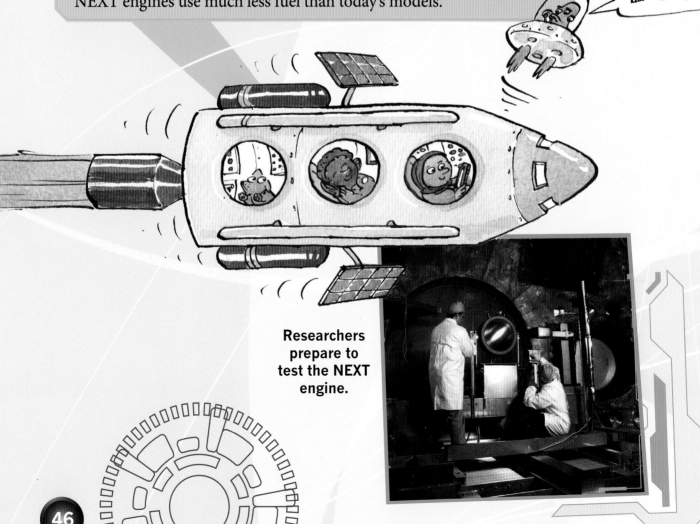

Researchers prepare to test the NEXT engine.

Okay, *Orion*!

There's also a new spacecraft ready to roll. The *Orion* is designed to take us farther than we've ever gone before—including all the way to Mars. Orion looks like the *Apollo* spacecraft that brought astronauts to the Moon in the 1960s and '70s, but it's bigger and better. There's a toilet (nicer than having to collect waste and release it into space on a cargo module), and there's room for more astronauts. But *Orion*'s still not roomy enough to live on for nine months, which is about how long it will take to get to Mars. Maybe the crew could hibernate while going there.

The *Orion*

Helping Hands

Getting into deep space—and staying there—will take cooperation. That's why 14 space agencies from around the world are working together in the International Space Exploration Coordination Group. Who's involved? Australia, Canada, China, the European Space Agency, France, Germany, India, Italy, Japan, the Republic of Korea, Russia, Ukraine, the United Kingdom, and the United States. That's a lot of helping hands!

Managers from different space agencies meet to discuss plans.

What's Next?

We may still be years away from living permanently in space, but don't let that stop you from dreaming about what life might be like "out there." New discoveries and technologies are being explored every day.

Pack Your Bags

Forget the beach—and imagine heading off to space on your next family vacation! A few companies are working hard to make that dream a reality. At first, your trip might involve just going high enough to experience a few minutes of zero gravity and to see the amazing curve of Earth. But the next step in space tourism could see the 25-year-old International Space Station turned into a hotel rather than retired. What's the expected price tag for this new type of luxury travel? Between $10 and $15 million. Start saving your allowance now!

Space traveler Anousheh Ansari trained for weeks before boarding the *Soyuz TMA-9* spacecraft bound for the ISS.

The exoplanet Ross 128 b was first spotted from the La Silla Observatory in northern Chile.

Exciting Exoplanets

Not so long ago, scientists could only explore other planets within our solar system. But thanks to new technologies, including stronger space telescopes and cameras, a whole new world has opened up. Exoplanets are located beyond our solar system, and a few of them might be able to support life.

Kepler-452b is the most Earth-like exoplanet ever discovered. It's located in the Goldilocks Zone of a star that's similar in size and temperature to our sun. And Ross 128 b—the latest exoplanet discovery—is about the same size as Earth and could have a similar surface temperature. Exciting news!

Keep Dreaming

Just as in the past, today's dreams will become tomorrow's realities as space explorers continue to invent technology that will allow us to go farther into space and stay longer. Will you be living on another planet one day? It could happen!

FURTHER READING

Aldrin, Buzz with Dyson, Marianne J. *Welcome to Mars: Making a Home on the Red Planet.* National Geographic Children's Books, 2015.

Flint, Katy. *Glow in the Dark: Voyage Through Space.* Quarto Publishing, 2018.

McNulty, Faith (Author) and Kellogg, Steven (Illustrator). *If You Decide to Go to the Moon.* Scholastic Press, 2005.

O'Brien, Patrick. *You Are the First Kid on Mars.* G. P. Putnam's Sons, 2009.

Vogt, Gregory L. *Is There Life on Other Planets?: and Other Questions about Space.* Lerner Publications, 2010.

Williams, Dave (Author), Cunti, Loredana (Author) and Krynauw, Theo (Illustrator). *Go for Liftoff!: How to Train Like an Astronaut.* Annick Press, 2017.

Williams, Dave (Author), Cunti, Loredana (Author) and Krynauw, Theo (Illustrator). *Mighty Mission Machines: From Rockets to Rovers.* Annick Press, 2018.

Williams, Dave (Author), Cunti, Loredana (Author) and Krynauw, Theo (Illustrator). *To Burp or Not to Burp: A Guide to Your Body in Space.* Annick Press, 2016.

IMAGE CREDITS

INDEX

Cover art/design by Pixel Hive Studio
Edited by Linda Pruessen
Designed by Pixel Hive Studio

We gratefully acknowledge and thank Dr. Parshati Patel, Outreach Program Coordinator at the Centre for Planetary Science and Exploration, Western University, for her ongoing encouragement, support, and feedback.

Annick Press Ltd.

We acknowledge the support of the Canada Council for the Arts and the Ontario Arts Council, and the participation of the Government of Canada/la participation du gouvernement du Canada for our publishing activities.

Funded by the Government of Canada | Financé par le gouvernement du Canada

ONTARIO ARTS COUNCIL
CONSEIL DES ARTS DE L'ONTARIO
an Ontario government agency
un organisme du gouvernement de l'Ontario

Cataloging in Publication
Williams, Dafydd, 1954-, author
Destination: space : living on other planets /
Dr. Dave Williams and Loredana Cunti.

(Dr. Dave Astronaut)
Issued in print and electronic formats.
ISBN 978-1-77321-057-5 (softcover).--ISBN 978-1-77321-058-2
(hardcover).--ISBN 978-1-77321-059-9 (PDF).--ISBN 978-1-77321-060-5
(EPUB)
1. Space colonies--Juvenile literature. 2. Habitable planets--
Juvenile literature. 3. Outer space--Civilian use--Juvenile literature.
4. Interplanetary voyages--Juvenile literature. I. Cunti, Loredana,
1968-, author II. Title. III. Series: Williams, Dafydd, 1954- . Dr. Dave Astronaut

TL795.7.W54 2018   j629.44'2   C2018-901034-7
C2018-901035-5

Published in the U.S.A. by Annick Press (U.S.) Ltd.
Distributed in Canada by University of Toronto Press.
Distributed in the U.S.A. by Publishers Group West.

Printed in China

www.annickpress.com

Also available as an e-book. Please visit www.annickpress.com/ebooks.html for more details.

This book is dedicated to all young readers who are curious about living in space and are unafraid to go farther and stay longer. Join in the future of space exploration and go for it!—D.W.

This is for my friends and family and all fellow Earth beings. As cool as it is thinking about life on other planets, only here do I have all of you to share a laugh with. —L.C.